GW01066299

PETE MULLINEAUX grew up in Bristol, UK. His poem *Harvest Festival*, published, aged 13, in Macmillan's anthology *Poetry & Song,* was subsequently recorded for schools by Harrap on the album *Man & His Senses.* Living in London in the 'alternative' late 1970s and early '80s – he worked in a left wing printing press and played in a punk rock band *The Resisters* – recording an album in 1979 on Munich's Trikont records. When the band split he went solo as singer-songwriter Pete Zero, with gigs ranging from two Glastonbury Festivals, CND protests at Greenham Common and Brockwell Park to sharing the stage with such diverse luminaries as the early Pogues and Salman Rushdie. His protest song *Disposable Tissues* in support of CND won the 1986 City of London Poetry/Song contest and he also published a collection of songs under the same title. Adapting to the emerging new comedy and performance poetry scenes he played host for alternative cabaret group *New Variety* in the Old White Horse in Brixton as well as performing with the London based *Apples & Snakes* – appearing in their first publication *Raw & Biting Cabaret Poetry.* (1985) His one man show – *The Performer's Fear of the Gong* – was described by *What's On* Magazine as 'A must!' Around this time he also achieved a first class honours in drama from Middlesex University, wrote for the Paul Merton fronted *Comedy Wavelength* (Channel 4) and a first stage play *Wallflowers* was produced on the London fringe.

A Father's Day
Pete Mullineaux

Best wishes
Pete Mullineaux

salmonpoetry

Published in 2008 by
Salmon Poetry,
Cliffs of Moher, County Clare, Ireland
Website: www.salmonpoetry.com
Email: info@salmonpoetry.com

ISBN 978-1-903392-87-4

Cover photograph: Pete Mullineaux
Cover design & typesetting: Siobhán Hutson

To my father

Acknowledgements

Acknowledgements are due to the editors of the following, in which some of these poems have been published:

Poetry Ireland Review, The Stinging Fly, The SHOp, ROPES, Crannog, Imagine, West 47, West 47 Online, Cuirt Journal & Annual, Anglo-Welsh Borderlines, Van Gogh's Ear, (France) *Nomad*, (Scotland) *Galway Now Magazine, Galway Advertiser, Poetry Now, Poetic License* (UK.)

Several poems also appeared in a pamphlet published by Lapwing, *Zen Traffic Lights* (2005).

Special thanks to Jessie Lendennie and Siobhán Hutson at Salmon and to Gerry Hanberry for going through the manuscript and sharing his enlightened thoughts.

Contents

am

pm

am

Father's Day

So here I am –
mid-day, mid-week, mid-life;
Easons, Galway; second floor:
looking for a greeting card
in the 'Father's Day' section;
which seems a touch small considering
how many there are in this world;
although in fairness, still only February –
off season for dads.

I become aware of a young man
selecting a Valentine, winking at me;
he probably thinks I'm only pretending
to buy a Father's Day card.
I try to reply with my eyebrows –
'No, you have it wrong
I really am looking for my father,
who is long dead.'

But he does it again several times
and I realise it's just a wink;
unless he's playing that murder game;
or else buying a card for himself.
I resume my search
hoping for one that says –
'Sorry, belated wishes'
but the messages are either
jokey or crude and I'm clearly
not in the winking mood.

I settle for a Valentine instead –
'I love you Dad!'
There, it's said.

Mowing

One hand on the throttle –
engine idling, he kicks
aside the coughed up grass

impeding his progress; continues
chewing blithely through
the last remaining stubble

of his days; until, finally;
the machine insists: stalls.
A moment of quiet –

the world stops turning
as my father bends low,
reaching into the mower

for the wet dark clumps
clinging to the moment.

Tonight's the Night

I took Dad to see Neil Young; he wore his suit (Dad, that is —
Neil Young wore a tie-dye shirt.)

1975 (I think) Bristol Colston Hall: crazy Neil with Crazy Horse.
And crazy me for bringing Dad

but he'd taken me to Cheddar caves, Castle Coombe, and over
on the ferry to South Wales —

(again, Dad, not Neil Young, who hadn't take me anywhere, yet.)
So I wanted to show him something,

even though his taste in music began and ended with Bing Crosby;
(definitely Dad, not Neil Young

whose influences would be well, more blues, roots country
and rock and roll.)

And he was cross: (Neil, this time; my dad was surprisingly
mellow, if somewhat conspicuous.)

They started with a brand new song called *Tonight's the Night*
which the audience heckled

wanting more familiar tunes like *Southern Man, Helpless*
and *Cowgirl in the Sand.*

But Neil was having none of it — he gave us all a lecture:
how this was about someone

real close to him, a roadie who had died from drugs —
'Bruce Berry was a working man ...'

and sang it again, only more aggressive; which pissed
the audience off even more.

I was hoping Dad was OK, not feeling out of place
but he seemed to be taking it all in

even nodding his silver head through the deranged
twenty minute guitar solos.

Eventually there was a compromise: the band
won us over by doing all the old hits

but then, for an encore did *Tonight's the Night* again.
I'll never forget it,

afterwards, he bought me a takeaway, (Dad, not Neil Young)
don't know what Neil and the band got up to

maybe they went back to the hotel
and talked about an old guy in the third from back row

who had smiled all through the concert,
and wondered what he was taking.

Whatever, I enjoyed myself too –
felt Dad and Neil Young

had got on well together.
'Bruce Berry was a working man ...'

Missing

Marking thirty years,
the Film Society's choice
set in Pincochet's Chile,
featured Jack Lemmon
as a bewildered father
searching for his daughter
and himself –
finding it hard to believe
things had got that bad.

I left the cinema
disorientated and terrified,
convinced I was being followed;
haunted by that scene
of a horse in the night
racing over the dark cobbles
out of control –

stumbled
into bed like a child;
succumbed to the fog of sleep;
thankful I could rest till morning,
that no-one would come
with an early call –
my mailbox would not be
stuffed to overflowing
with blank postcards.

Keeping Terrorists at Bay

The Guantanamo inmates are writing poems, (why not,
guests also enjoy cricket, baseball and Irish dancing,)
– putting it all down, with sharpened pencils
making marks you can see, on paper that doesn't lie.
Despite all the free time, the scribbling is frenzied,
some detainees compose automatically, even in sleep.
One epic alone has a thousand stanzas and the writer
knows them by heart, (they have never left the heart.)
A few shorter verses have even been published.

There are boundaries to this generous dispensation:
prisoners are not allowed to communicate. The poem
must not carry a message intended for other ears.
This is too wishy-washy; let us make it even clearer:
a poem cannot be aimed at an identifiable target.
One opus has been intercepted and destroyed
because it addressed the writer's mother: beginning,
'Dear Mother.' Remember, these people are devious,
they do not know the ropes or understand restraint;
deceptive ramblings may contain hidden devices,
guiding the reader towards subversive meaning.

You have to know the code to see between the lines,
it's a cultural thing and the hard-pressed authorities
employ special censors, trained to spot clues.
Even here you cannot be too careful, who can tell:
perhaps some in secret are poets themselves?
It is hard not to be swayed by the power of words.
As a precaution our line-detectors and semantic nit-pickers
are relieved from front line duty at regular intervals,
to avoid battle fatigue: the possibility of seduction.

The prisoners are not as innocent as they claim.
Believe us, we have had to discover the hard way,
some poems are heat-seeking and know their purpose;
others step up, clothed in a bland conformity,
so you drop your guard and wave them through
only to find they carry a hidden payload ...

There is an imperceptible pause, a nano-second
when you are neither hot nor cold; north, south, east or west;
alive or dead; before all becomes crystal-clear
as the words literally explode in your face:
or worse still, inside your head.

A Hug a Hug ...

I needed a BIG one –
unfortunately, right
at that critical moment,
God's hands were tied.

Jesus kept his arms
outstretched, possibly
overwhelmed –
surprised to see me.

Adam took forever:
switching off the mower,
emptying the grass tray,
taking his gloves off.

I queued with the rest
for Mother Amma,
who gave me her best
but I had to share her with the whole world!

The Buddha offered
a smile that said –
'Don't get too attached.'
Cruel to be kind.

And so I grabbed a tree,
which held firm –
if a little stiff –
like those other times

we do the tree hug: formal,
pat on the back moments;
before going our separate ways ...
Oh puffed up universe!

– what price a big grizzly
right now, to say it will all be fine –
despite the carnage and doomsday predictions –
'There there it's OK, it's OK ...'

Men Knitting

after Lorca

The men are hard at it, knitting
hats scarves and gloves
for a blood wedding.

Prolonged engagement: sitting
in hired rooms; push and shove.
The men are hard at it, knitting

the same pattern; no quitting,
inexorably the cord rises above
for a blood wedding

to end all seasons; as hard-hitting
comrades line up like collared doves.
The men are hard at it, knitting

by firesides and bonfires spitting
hot confetti: making the most of
'A Blood Wedding'.

While up the road, they're fitting
fresh coils of razor wool, with love.
Blood wedding, the men are hard at it
knitting…

Superstrings

After 'Zeros & Ones' by Sadie Plant

OK, show me the ropes:
but first let them be untwined
to reveal supple interlace
of hemp, or hair –
finest filaments,
pliable but weight-bearing,

for here is a yarn less travelled,
our first great inventors
of weave, warp, weft –
whose lips were sealed
while deft fingertips
teased out infinity
from variable combinations

– grasp Ariadne's thread,
linkage back to inter-face
of loom and web, wonder of pattern;
first matrix: those spider-women
who gave us *bundle, tie, plait* and *knit*
whose opposable thumbs
taught how to hold, not hit

– and loosen those Gordian knots,
not with Alexander's trigger-blade
'cut the crap' crudity –
show the disarming nudity
of ropes gently uncoiled; a world less
blind and afraid.

How far back can we unravel?
How long have we been on the ropes?
How wonderful is a piece of string.

Drawing a Line

(Italian Prime Minister, Silvio Berlusconi, once ordered the removal of surrounding clothes lines, prior to an E.U. conference, saying the sight of women's underwear was distasteful. Meanwhile, a recent survey has revealed the domestic chore most loathed by men is hanging out the washing.)

Content enough, or so it seems, down at the machine –
one on one, at the very heart of the domestic scrum;
hunky on our hunkers – a packet of BOLD held up
to say, 'We won the cup!' And if we choose to play it rough,
isn't there that bullfight ad, where the guy goes mad

rolls in the mud to save his jeans before his blood?
So why not parade it? Surely a row of sun-dried denims
hanging free: raw, spicy, tex-mex; signalling exotic sex,
no messing with this high plains rolling drifter.
But no – you have to draw the line somewhere.

For now we come to the delicate things in life:
those belonging to the girlfriend or the wife.
Perhaps to be caught out there, broad daylight –
pegs between the teeth; bras, knickers waving in the breeze:
we feel unease ...

As if another man, sidling by in disbelief, might see
how we've been trapped and tamed; shamed –
flying the flags of our intimacy; *her* territory:
hung out to dry – lonesome cowboy holding
a fistful of clothesline.

Though strangely enough, she likes to linger,
holding up our Y-fronts, boxers, jocks –
declaring loud and clear 'My husband's socks!'
brazen as the gold ring on her finger.
You have to draw a line somewhere.

Goose v Gander

On our kitchen table
back in the 1970's
a brown bottle
of *Daddies Sauce*.

It sort of went with chips
and sort of didn't –
too much spice
better suited to mash and peas.

Not surprisingly
there was a family joke
that it was specially
made for our Dad.

Mother, to be contrary
saw red –
preferring
Heinz or HP.

Power Cut

We cannot see ...
      instant NIGHT –

a mad scramble for matches –
hands claw, flounder
on unfamiliar surfaces; strangers to touch.

Using memory as compass
locate bearings, establish base camp,
      re-settle…
gradually become accustomed
to haloes, shadow selves –
we eat by candlelight, faces like glow-worms;
the children in ecstasy, no homework!

Then later, gathered around an open fire,
tuned in to the absolute hush –
even the fridge hum extinguished;
stoking the silence reverently, filling
it only with our heartbeats:
a universe ticking –

And imagining this could be

         'THE END'

tell fond stories from when we were young,
and still younger –
a time when God lived in the sky
Santa came down the chimney, and look,
up there – through wisps of smoke
an inverted well-shaft –
fairy lights dancing on dark water;
sparkling cellophane…

a spot of rain —
and down below
creation fizzles in a log burning.

At times like these we know
there has to be life on other planets:
are we not visitors ourselves —
far from home?

      Then —

      LIGHT!

And there is the cave, just as we left it.

Power restored.

Normality resumes, and yet
a strange relief, as if the universe
really had been holding its breath;
and despite the obligatory hoorays
for a few critical moments
something in us remains apart —
reluctant to come forward;
those shadows on the wall,
clawing their way back slowly;
curiously ambivalent.

Bar Codes

Each Zebra
has a distinctive stripe pattern –
a survival mechanism,

when lions attack
and the hooves scatter –
for a split sec
                ond

the swirling shapes are
                too mes merising
                        for selection

                of any o
                                ne
                                    in di vi du al…

A lion
is only faster
over a short distance

by the time
it makes a choice
the zebras are   moreoftenthannot   gone.

I'm thinking this
as I stare down
the supermarket aisle,
trying to remember
what I came in for…

An Old Corner Store

Come, enter if we dare
this cluttered, yet ordered interior;
purchasing a simple ball of string,
a chocolate bar, we invite close scrutiny:
no CCTV, but the watchful eye
of the proprietor following us
into the dark labyrinth; awaiting
our heroic return to the great counter –
a ritualistic passing of each chosen article
from hand to hand and back again to hand;
so too with the payment –
an operation of grave and delicate intimacy;
hence the cordial conversation.

But, once out in the open air –
inspecting the twine to find it in knots,
our chocolate bar glued to the wrapper –
we curse our innocence!
How long must they have lingered
on those dusty lower shelves
in dark despair; awaiting their deliverance,
our opportune arrival?

One small corner of the globe
will never be the same, as we turn
to demand compensation –
face the disarming 'ding' of the door,
then a puzzled frown as each offending object
is sifted once again from hand to hand –
caressed like a rare jewel; lifted up to the light,
as if to check for a serial number, a water line?

When replacements are finally offered
from the same musty shelves
and the claustrophobic darkness thickens,
it's getting hard to breathe…

So step into the bright new Tescos!
Blissful anonymity: announcements
Like a holiday camp – 'Good morning
Shoppers!' Here we feel welcomed
But unfussed, the cheery voice a good
Arms length away: permission to wander
Round and round for endless lifetimes;
Our trolleys for company; no problem
Returning that twine or chocolate bar,
They have trillions! Although we might
Prefer the aisles to be a little more ne
Gotiable, and – where does the time go?

The pace quickens –
as approaching the checkout
in a sudden urge to leave,
or heave; sixth sensing our souls,
our very lives are at risk;
fearing we may have stayed
too long in Tir na nÓg –
will exit past our sell-by date;
praying to God there isn't a queue –
why is the one in front always so slow!

Do we not recognise
that familiar stooped figure
counting out loose change;
who has brought along
their own bottomless basket;

now calling a stop –
insisting we mark this occasion
with some dallying and polite words;
recognition of our convergence:
some thoughtful wrapping around the time
as each prized item is passed
from hand to hand and back again to hand;
mutual smiles of appreciation
for the prices paid, the great distance travelled;
just how far we have had to come.

Slides

1

Before I could swim in the deep
end of the pool, at the bottom
of the big slide, the top half
of my father bobbed in the
water, arms outstretched
ready to catch me;
which he did

every time.

2

At home we had a stair bannister,
overburdened with coats
which were always
falling on the floor:
school mornings
he'd pick them
up, car engine
running –

out of his depth.

Gone Fishing

I

Somewhere off the coast of sanity
he is cut adrift; all at sea.

Scrambling towards safety
I secure a tenuous foothold –

turn to scan the rocks below
for shape and meaning;

send out my belated search party,
umbilical rope dangling;

hoping to see an orange flare;
a figure in a yellow dingy, calling –

'Over here you fool!'

II

Perhaps he has crawled
out from the water
like a castaway,

swings in a hammock
made from vines,
smelling of coconut oil;

walking the island
I test my own footprints,
hear his voice in damp caves,

the whispering surf;
rising sorrow
of oyster-catchers.

III

The mind combs
shores of unreason
for a sheltered cove,
a safe landing point;
finds instead
makeshift buoyancy
of a hospital bed,
tossing in the shallows:
no sirens or mermaids,
only starched indifference
of gull-like nurses
exhausted from constant flight;
a ward sister praying
through the night
that death will take him,
not just for his own sake,
but everyone concerned;
as if having lost his way
he is good as gone already;
a small lapse then
to leave the cabin window open,
let in the cold night air.

The consultant is discreet,
moves us away from the other wrecks;
explains how anchors will come loose
in a storm ...
        I want to lash out,
puncture and sink his sorry lifeboat,
but like everyone else
he is only doing his best
to keep us all afloat.

IV

I still see my father
wandering the wards,
caught in his own maelstrom;
a lost Odysseus,
negotiating jutting reefs –
other more perilous hazards;
sharing meandering tales
with fellow shipwrecked sailors.

After a lifetime saying little
now he can't stop talking,
a great speech, saved up too long
overflowing its containment,
pouring out drunkenly
in all directions.

V

But in his very last moments
either the ocean has dried up
or else the drugs have finally taken hold;
he says nothing, grips my wrist
as if this might be an oar –
something more solid
than the condemned raft;
indicating he needs to pee ...

We would have liked full sail,
but with no screens available
or nurse in sight
I do my best to steer him
into the metal jug.

We haven't touched hands
since childhood –
now he is the child,
me the father,
our fingers meshed
on the quivering tiller;
as we head for open sea –
calm after the storm,
clear water ...

Playing Boats

for Cassie

Running for the river
she barely breaks her stride
to pluck a yellow dandelion;
while I take time to choose
a broad, tapering leaf –
not too green.

And here we come!
her in front, approaching the first fall.
Down ... under; then up she bobs –
snagging on a rock
while I career on into calmer waters.

But now she's wriggling, and free!
Rotating, gathering momentum
until we're finally neck and neck –
father and daughter, sailing up the Nile, the Amazon.

A whirlpool –
now I'm in difficulties
taking in water, while she shoots clear.
We watch, cheek to cheek
until her yellow head disappears
beneath overhanging trees ...

Am I sad my boat sank? She asks.

The rules are simple: if both get stuck
we throw stones to dislodge ourselves
or run ahead, removing obstacles.
But what if one fails to make the start:
will our game not then be over?

Come on, she coaxes, chiding
my dark cloud, swiping another flower
holding it under my chin.

This time I seek a fresher,
more robust leaf.
Best of three, I say –
let's see that dandelion spin!

Twinned

You're about to be born,
approaching entry –
feeling pampered;
having percolated
nine soft months
in a pool of natural juices;
a silken cord
offers elastic security,
once you make that
trusting leap
into a world
patiently awaiting
your arrival.

Now your twin.

Shaky in this other cell,
your host forever on the move;
along with a cocktail
of drugs, killer bugs
her agitation prepares
for red alert.
When the order comes
you will parachute in
under cover of darkness
tugging frantically at your own cord;
hide the evidence of arrival
in the undergrowth –
enter a world
that awaits you too
with open arms.

In Our Hands

For as long as anyone could remember
(and a few were hitting nine and ten)
the end of the cul-de-sac had been our playground.
A jungle of scrub, bed-springs, old tyres;
here we re-made history according to the movies:
Ben Hur, Spartacus, The Guns of Navarone!

Now they were putting in new garages.
And for a while the huge diggers were a novelty:
became Chieftain tanks, Hannibal's elephants;
we even got to ride like Caesars in the toothed bucket;
each fresh mound of earth offering dizzier heights,
visions of grandeur, until, reality dawned –
we were the barbarians.

Up went the barbed-wire fence, a 'keep out' sign;
then a flattening of innocence, as we watched
laying of concrete, building blocks; unrolling of roof felt;
tried to console our impotence with cheerful taunts
of 'slave labour' – but the metamorphosis continued.

Finally the windows: timber frames, panes of glass, and
then something grey-blue, opaque; malleable ...

> Putty! This was the stuff: a potent weapon
> made for guerrilla warfare –
> we slid our fingers along the ledges,
> dug out handfuls, saw who could make the biggest ball.

The windows fell out, but what did we care?
These garages were colonising our land,
were we not outlaws – freedom fighters?
There in our shaking hands –
fistfuls of dynamite.

The Chair

A quiet man, unobtrusive;
once tucked in he became invisible.
And though we might occasionally
sink into the worn upholstery,
it was only for my father
the chair agreed to work its special charms,
wrapping him in snug arms
offering safe harbour.

My mother in contrast was everywhere:
perpetual motion, like a fish.
'Your supper's on the table.'
'I think I'll eat it on my lap,' he'd reply,
heading for his retreat.

Sundays: the doldrums,
metallic skies of dull chrome.
The family dinner over, I'd sneak out,
leaving him in his usual place,
her for once becalmed, sprawled
on the settee like Eartha Kitt –
watching the box, doped on tedium.

When the cat got in and peed
all over Dad's chair,
my mother took the excuse
to have the thing thrown out.

That evening, gathered like porpoises,
or sharks around a raft,
we witnessed a rare moment;
akin to a death, or the sighting of land,

when he seemed for once
wholly visible, hesitating –
as if expecting the world to right itself,

before paddling sideways
to the bare rock
where my mother lay like a siren
in her best Carmen curlers –
waiting.

Passenger from Hell

Ticket in hand
a window seat,
there in time
to avoid the queue
already backing
down the street –
been to the loo,
packed only
the bare essentials,
you tilt on back
stretch those weary
existentials ...
breathe a sigh
dig in.

So far so good –
sandwiches
book
flask of tea
last night's dreams
for company
it's all as it was
meant to be.

Not too phased
when a minute to go
a palpable rise
in passenger flow
as last chancers
scramble aboard
some full of talk
some weighed down
unable to walk –

young, old
someone with
a heavy cold –
'That should be in the hold'
you mumble,
taking up space,
getting in with
the first grumble.

Now play Big Brother
buried behind
your hardback
cover, smile at those
you know are passing by –
leave nothing to chance
discerning ones
will tell at a glance
from your choice
of Virginia Wolf
you need
room.

None the less,
lids half-closed,
coat draped across
the adjacent seat
(the star prize)
your antennae
keep a vigil
for innocent souls
who might mistake
a non committal stare
for The Good Samaritan,
remain seemingly
distracted,
unaware –

you let an invisible
flag declare —
keep off the grass,
otherwise engaged,
leave me alone!

No morality here
the truth is
you need it,
to them it's only a luxury
to you it's health,
life, death —
some may want to share
their hopes and dreams
holiday snaps,
magazines —
it's a free world.

Anyway —
fingers crossed
prayers said,
you're purring,
practically putting
yourself to bed
as the doors begin to close
with that so exquisite
'hisssssssssss' —
(surely a sound
made by the gates of heaven)
sealing you safely
into bliss ...
you can now afford
a sorry smile for
those who must remain,
left stranded in the rain,
those who will have to
wait.

But ...
just as you felt most secure
through the barest hair-width
aperture –
with immaculate timing
dare-devil ease
a squeeze ...
            and he's in:

your nemesis –
your virtual passenger from hell;
graphic description must wait
for fear of under-emphasis;
the immediate task is evasive action,
turning your neck just a fraction
without delay
quickly scan the state of play ...

and see you've truly cooked your goose,
all seats are now occupied –
that is except for <u>one</u>.

Too late for remorse!
you could have chosen
the woman with the fold-up pram
now packed away,
her five kids thumbs in mouths
quiet as mice;
the elderly one
you thought would
lend you her advice
has fallen asleep;
that nun from Clare
that refugee
the fellow with the beer belly,
had you but known
it listed to the left!

new-agers connected
by their rings
teen lovers
by their tongues,
a tourist in a bulky
Arran sweater;
even the busker
with the juggling clubs
and didgeridoo
would have been better.

But no –
you're stuck, squirming
like Prufrock on his pin
exposed as they say in spades
all shades of pink
the jilted lover
staring down the aisle –

as Balor's eye
radars in ...
picks out that vacant space within –
the probing searchlight says,
'What's wrong with you?'
You want to shout
'It was my choice ...'

but too long staying mum –
your voice tails off in a whisper
lost in the rumbling engine
thrum.

So now –
picture the worst scenario
as he sits, legs splayed
knees wide open
not to mention the mouth

snoring all the way –
by the time you reach
your destination
you will intimately
know those gums
have every filling
marked on your brain
like an X ray;
as the fingers twitch
searching pockets
for unknown horrors –
a packet of fags
the fizzy drink
that has jumped up and down
to get here
waiting to be sprayed
in your direction;
or the tin-foil baguette
sealed for days
allowed to sweat,
awaiting its aromatic
unveiling…

Sure enough –
the slimiest rasher and ripest egg
hit you full on the nose
you reach up
for the air conditioner
only to nudge an elbow –
turn the galvanised
grin towards you –
get full frontal view
of crunching molars
slicing blades
Jaws One, Two, Three
all possible sequels –

then, holding the wretched thing
suspended
mid-swallow ...
he'll tumble off to sleep
as the rumble of the road takes over
leaning slowly but surely
on to your hard shoulder.

But no –
a light begins to shine
the dawning of a day:
not a dream or April fool,
a miracle!
You shake your frazzled wits
in a glorious 'hallelujah!' –
you've escaped
you're a survivor –
he's taking the only other possible seat ...

he's the driver.

Zen Traffic Lights

Thank you red dragon
for teaching patience and humility,
so I may observe the green tiger
wisely.

And thank you red dragon
for showing joy in the moment;
so I will ride the green tiger
with enhanced pleasure.

And thank you red dragon
for reflecting my rage, mirrored
in calm cool green waters
to come,

Thank you ...
thank you ...
that's enough now,

THANK YOU!

pm

Paradise Let Go

Somehow, despite good intentions
we cannot quite regain
the ground we seem to have lost.

Boosted by latest inventions
we surge ahead like trains
of thought, those good intentions

until someone mentions
the war, or rather wars – again.
Then we do seem lost

for ideas: despite pretensions,
our umbrellas in the rain;
those good intentions.

But while doubts and tensions
may always remain,
perhaps all is not lost –

it might not require abstentions
to ease eternal pain:
once we abandon (misplaced) intentions
by now, as good as lost.

Father's Day Reprise

The next time I'm in Easons
I hang around downstairs
for a while, browsing

through Dante's *Inferno*;
so I feel more buoyed and cheerful,
up and ready for it –

ascend the escalator relaxed,
as in the *Paradiso* –
a smile on my face,

(I can tell because
today I stand still and allow the
moving metal to carry me.)

I get to the top and bump into the back
of another man
who has stopped dead:

he seems afraid to get off
and is back-pedalling
as fast as he can ...

it's like a moonwalk routine
and I have to do it too.
I feel hands on my hips

and now there is
a line of us, in a conga
all moondancing –

'One small step'
the man said
but this one is huge!

We stretch out into the street,
passers-by think it's a parade
practising for Paddy's Day,

but no this is for Fathers Day;
we have all come to pay our
tributes and respects.

Now the security guard
is taking the man at the front
in his arms

lifting him to safety,
bearing him like a lover;
a hug to die for.

Then it's a rush
to buy our cards;
one fellow is ancient,

he looks like Rip Van Winkle,
white beard dragging on the floor.
'Surely your father can't be still alive?' I say.

He tells me the card is for himself,
he buys several every year
one from each of his children.

'Are they all dead?' I ask.
'To me,' he replies.
I say nothing –

we are all searching for our fathers
reaching for the right words;
an appropriate image:

there are pictures of golf, football,
I'm hoping for a lawnmower
and am amazed to find one

but the message inside
puts me off; too religious –
after all, it's my own father I'm looking for.

I try to visualise
a wheelbarrow
a red one ...

I'm almost settling for an empty chair,
when I spot something –
the message says:

'Well done – you've passed your test!'
And I realise I've wandered
into another section

and suddenly feel dizzy
sensing one more false move
I could be falling through hoops

into MacNeice's *Soap Suds*
or take a wrong turn
and end up like Dante

in a nightmare parallel world
where the cards read:
'Hard luck – you failed'

'Miserable Birthday'
'Christmas condolences'
'Commiserations on your wedding.'

I realise that I'm being observed,
there is a man eyeing me
from behind the stationary –

it isn't the security guard
because he's still giving bear hugs
to needy fathers stepping off the escalator;

 (I'm thinking that Easons
should give him
a pay rise at least.)

No, this man looks like a cold war spy,
tough and uncompromising,
I notice his umbrella has a sharp point.

I know why he is here –
he has been sent by my father
to see if I am buying him a card.

I return my attention to the greetings,
perhaps I will choose
a funny one after all?

'Sorry Dad I forgot
to buy you a card
– Ha ha!'

Dad rhymes with sad,
mad, glad, cad, bad and
had?

Knock knock!
Who's there?
Dad: Dad who?

But now, as if a hooter has sounded,
we grab our cards
descend the stairs en masse –

(there is no down escalator in Easons Galway
'We will take you up but
you will have to bring yourself down'

a strange subliminal message)
– and there is the security guard
back in his spot by the door

flexing his lips and eyebrows
as if nothing has happened
staring straight ahead, like men do at urinals,

I imagine it's part of the training;
and I know that everything
is back to normal

the next person getting a bear hug
will be some poor soul who has
in a moment of weakness

failed to pay for his copy of
New Scientist, DIY Weekly
or *Men's Health*.

Outside the buskers are playing
the rain is falling
and I feel a sudden urge

to shake hands
with a man coming towards me,
a complete stranger

I'm thinking 'why not?'
I will offer my hand
before we end up killing each other.

746

for Dermot Desmond:
746th in the Forbes rich list

It isn't fair –
As Ryan Tubridy joked on the radio,
'Who wants to be 746th at anything?'

What's another billionaire?
When to think: a touch more generous,
a grand or two less needy,

I'd be 747…

Now there's a number that rings,
to have you walking on air,

I might have had wings!

Lifted

(after Longfellow's Hiawatha)

Out of hazy mists of morning,
following the yellow tramlines,
by the kerb side with a shuffle,
ready with the open note-book,
came the terrible traffic warden;
gazing into frosted windows,
searching for the disc of safety;
quick to spot when one was missing,
quick to write and wave the ticket;
slip it in behind the wipers –
there for all the world to witness;
see the misdemeanour punished,
see the smile of one returning
folding like a concertina –
in time to see the clamper's lorry
lifting with a fist of iron
this year's model BMW…

Chequered Flag

What's a dodgy fuel pump,
worn gaskets, a knackered
distributor, when –

browsing through magazines
in the doctor's surgery,
awaiting your annual NCT

you see in *Top Gear*
that despite a lawnmower engine,
60mph speed limit

and being out of production
for thirty odd years, leaving
the Aston Martin DBS

smarting, Maserarti
Quattroporto
gutted –

the modest Fiat 500
still gets the vote
for sexiest car ever.

Sitting pretty
at the front of the grid,
suddenly

you feel a lot better –
tempted to tell the doctor
you're fixed.

Mechanic

(i.m. Pat Maloney – Shrue, Co Galway.)

A banjaxed exhaust, a worn clutch,
he'd never charge an arm or leg
even when the job was long and messy.
As for knowledge; not just the makes,
he knew all their faults and defects;
took one look at our Opel Corsa:
'Goes through wipers like a man though tea' –
then got us through the NCT.

Alone in that barn of a garage,
cold whistling in off the lake
he somehow filled the place with warmth;
tools lay around like shrapnel –
'It's here somewhere,' he'd say
looking a touch lost himself
while your little car felt right at home.

Among the wrecks abandoned
to his care – an old Volks Beetle:
forever fiddling with it, 'One day.'
And true, he could take forever –
driving neighbours into town,
sorting out every passing enquiry.
At least he had no phone.

As the hearse pulled up,
(which no doubt he'd fixed some time)
and the crowd moved in –
you half expected his legs
to be sticking out from underneath:
hear him call your name

in recognition of your shoes,
your cough; the signature hack
and sputter of your car.

'We'll be at those plugs now,'
you wanted him to say,
except his heart gave way;
suddenly –
like a jack.

How's the Old Ticker?

Great watch you have there
capturing your wrist: jewels,
anti-rust, water resistant.

I could reveal mine – cost?
Two euro: but I keep it in my pocket
because the plastic strap broke

and anyway, I'd rather display
the twenty four carat heart
leaping
        from
               my
                    sleeve!

Group Hug at the Men's Weekend

We're trying not to move –
clinging to this moment like limpets;
mussels at low tide, letting juices
trapped inside go deeper still,
with each salt lick and lapping motion ...

Oceans to fathom, but then I hear it:
a whisper –
'Make something happen'

And fearing perhaps the moon
may swoon and sigh; turn a blind eye
to our efforts – forget to spin the tide
and leave us stranded here; facing in
like Easter Island statues ...

'Maintain the flow' – that voice again.
I gently release and set myself adrift –
instantly a wave, uplift – flight! High I go
into the clouds, a glimpse of gold ...

      Then 'plop' –
like a lead shot, I drop, back
into the primal muck, now a spiralling
ruck of clinging foot-tongues singing!

hell bent –
I try to slow the inevitable descent.

Later, the moment passed, evaporated –
I venture to point out the 'men' in mo*men*tum.
Someone else notes a *mom* and *tum*.
We all get pats on the back.

Time to go, one or two linger, unsure –
I'm offered a parting squeeze on the forearm,
around the muscle; light enough to do no harm,
set off no more alarm.

Hamnet

*Shakespeare rarely saw his son Hamnet, (who died age 12)
spending most of the child's brief life working away from home.*

I

It had to be worth it –
Macbeth, Lear and the rest;
would have been impossible
what with colic, night feeds
the challenge of always
coming up with a bed time story.

II

But I return now as a ghost,
spinning a sorry tale
to keep you awake,
provide some manly motivation:
remember me; avenge me –
(blame your mother!)

III

If I could wave my wand again:
after the unavoidable shipwreck
perhaps this time I'd bring you with me
to that magic isle.

Baking Blind

This fatherhood thing is hell –
changing nappies and baking pastry
sure don't gel.

OK, I agree,
typical man,
looking for sympathy –

the TV's
on for a start,
an obvious distraction.

Actually ... it's the Olympics,
look –
a Russian in the decathlon:

event five – the pole vault;
technique without a fault;
now there's a real all-rounder!

And on the high board,
a Chinese girl, (someone's daughter)
offers reverse handstand with tuck

and triple jack-knife somersault –
opening at the very last second,
to part the obliging water.

Oh fuck, the blackberries!
pouring purple lava
down the oven ...

'Sorry love, won't be a second,
yes, I know you've made a mess as well –
hold on ...'

I think of the old one across the way:
when life was tough, how did she do it?
A dozen at least, or so they say

reared without disposables
or washing machine;
fed on home-made everything.

Surely there were moments
when the neighbours heard her scream,
'Enough!'

There she is now –
out in her garden, mowing
an already immaculate lawn;

stifling a yawn: effortless –
she could do it blindfold;
her mind is even somewhere else.

Is that the secret –
was it ever not?

Madonna!

(as the Italians say it)

Such tenderness, even in stone –
the master's soft touch: mother
and child, inseparable; carved
from the same immortal block.

But please, come closer...
I have to whisper, not move my lips:
I couldn't bear another miracle –
the crowds are bad enough already.
Yet I must tell someone...

I'm just not sure it's me somehow –
this everlasting motherhood.
I only seem weighed down by it all,
the awesome responsibility;
the endless questioning, his constant
fidgeting and jockeying in my lap
forcing me to say things like –
'You'll fall...'

But then he cocks his little head
smiles up so disarmingly, reminding me
he has his future; deftly chiselled features
chiding my self-importance. He turns
my cheek towards his: knows it all already –
(I wonder – had it been a girl?)

Look closely, the cracks are there:
fault lines in the mould –
I can feel their seismic grating
announcing his departure. No doubt

he will leave a consoling kiss
on this weary forehead
telling me not to worry – it will
all work out, one way or another.

And of course he'll keep in touch...

Another Madonna

She grips her baby with one arm –
removes the morning clutter; puts back the milk,
re-seals the butter

as coughing fit to choke,
carrying the paper and a smoke; he enters –
life's companion: her bloke.

Scans the room with vacant eyes –
takes in a shape
he seems to recognise –

offering a nod, a grunt –
enough to say
he bears the brunt

drifts off to some other place;
his inner world,
her outer space.

Dances on Eggshells

For years B walked around
on eggshells: fearing A's cold shoulder,
or else the indifferent sideswipe,
the casual malice.

Until one day B finally said, 'Enough'
took the poker from the fire,
shoved it in A's face –
'Come on you bastard.'

A went out for a few drinks.
Later B got a call from the guards
to say A had been found in a puddle
comatose.

B didn't know what to do,
so took the kids to the cinema,
to be alone, lost in the dark –
protected by the silver light.

The film was *Dances with Wolves*,
with lots of fighting and dying: there was
a white girl brought up by Indians
who had been given a new name.

This is it then, B thought –
new beginning, a new me.
From now on I will be called…

Dances on eggshells.

Patsy Panda at the Schoolbook Reunion

Hi, it's me, Patsy…Patsy Panda –
remember that first book at school?
Patsy Panda & Huggy Bear…

Yeah, cool – we were there!

I suppose it was nice to share
even if you did have that other one
all to yourself – *Get up Huggy!*

But hey, what a bear.

We were the tops, till along came
Danny Dinosaur and *Harry Hedgehog;*
Huggy is a Rascal, Huggy at the Shops.

Me? Oh I stuck around somewhere
got covered in lipstick – advanced horseplay;
things move on quick, don't they.

Strange I had no-one to myself anymore –
a girlfriend might have been nice
even for the odd row.
Still, adults know best: they know the score.

What does it matter – I'm all grown up now,
I imagine the girls in the class are too.
We mature quicker than boys – teacher said:
must be true!

> *Come on Huggies!*
> *Listen to your mammies:*
> *take off those trousers –*
> *put on your pyjamies!*

Early for School

for Gerry Hanberry

Silent corridors
cold radiators
empty classrooms

each closed door
begs a question
as mischievous

voices in the pipes
whisper
all the wrong answers

– drift
into the staff room
find myself

amidst charts
duties
role-calls

absentees
from days gone by

      a shuffle

in the hallway
chains of laughter
echoing

swish
of wand
and gown

more guests arriving…

Gallery

Even the red roped barriers impress.

Safe in the Louvre café
I comfort myself with a french pastry.

Next time: half a chance,
just one awesome frame ...

beneath which it all comes back:
Wednesdays; art class, double-period,

teacher leaning over one shoulder;
saying nothing,

(a cough perhaps)

moving on.

Male Nude: intermittently standing (unique)

And so to the climax of our visit –
this bold and challenging exhibit: immediately we ask ourselves,
what is it?

Clearly some form of installation: post modern, abstract –
representation?

One senses journey, transition –
something present by omission: inconclusive –
the meaning tantalisingly elusive ...

Deliberately ambiguous: observe the semi-solid material –
sensual, tactile; the lines appear vigorous, yet
the overall effect remains ethereal ...

Pornographic, depending on the light?

Performance piece: it seems to invite participation,
interaction –
        oh, sensation: transaction – elevation!
            heavens, what a climber...

and so witty –
        ah, that is a pity ...
            But here we go again!
                It must be on a timer.

So let's make a start: is this art?
A few guide notes might not go amiss –
unless it's simply taking the piss.
Certainly we can all agree
this has to be the star attraction –
the sheer reaction it's provoking;
no end of poking!

So congratulations to the artist,
(who unfortunately couldn't be here)
such total lack of inhibition;
certainly making an exhibition.

(But where to put the red dot –
it isn't clear ...)

The Bigger Picture

From *'Raincoat Drawing'* by Juan Munoz
in the Tate Modern Art Gallery, London

A room: white chalk
on grey-black canvas;
nothing is happening.

All is still: a table, a chair,
neutral furnishings
betray no emotion,

and yet
there is sadness –
something has occurred,

or is about to commence;
and standing here
at this particular moment,

you are both
early
and late.

But wait –
(you hadn't noticed)
a drawing hangs in the room;

you can just make out figures,
implicit movement;
suggestion of a narrative –

realise how desperately
you want to be in this frame
within a frame

safe from the terror
of the bigger picture.

Coming Back Down

(after Frost)

I haul my toboggan up the hill ...
a way to go, and oh so slow;
but that of course is snow.

I put my hands together and blow,
I have the urge, the will; I must
get to the top ...

then stop. For this is why I came
so perilously high –
to brush these clouds in communion;

greet the rising sun, then ...
know the thrill
of going down!

But, here I am the clown:
the journey up took far too long;
now the run is past – and gone.

And that of course is snow –
I know, I know.

Here Still

(a movement in parallel thirds)

Thinking
        staring at the wall
                searching palms

am I
        boring a hole
                cannot touch

still
        trying to see
                it would mean reaching

here
        beyond the pattern
                across

with them
        perhaps the chair
                a desert

in my splendid isolation
        could be moved
                a mountain range

the days sometimes pass
        closer to the window
                a wall of cut-glass

within reach
        a view of late summer flowers
                the risk is too great

a sail flutters
        still in bloom
                the distance too far

only to disappear
        still in colour
            the world

over the horizon
        still
                too

like a sunset
        here
                unsteady

Wasting Away

We hope that some things cannot be erased,
(the Buddhist sees each sorry soul return)
though most of it will have to go to waste.

Hooked on progress, forever making haste
we gobble up, incinerate and burn;
believing some things cannot be erased.

And for fear we may become debased,
we cultivate improvement; seek to learn:
though most of it will have to go to waste.

But whether we're the chaser or the chased,
much like a coin – depending on the turn;
hoping that some things cannot be erased

we look back at those footprints barely paced;
ley lines of meaning wistfully discern ...
though most of it will have to go to waste.

Thinking then of this life as but a taste
of things to come; beyond our current concern:
accepting we will one day be erased –
we hope (and pray) that some things never go to waste.